BUD'S INSTRUCTION MANUAL

Learn More then the Basics about

Janitorial, Floor Maintenance, Carpet Cleaning, Office Cleaning and More

How to Start Your Own Business at a Low Cost

Bloomington, IN Milton Keynes, UK
authorHOUSE®

AuthorHouse™
1663 Liberty Drive, Suite 200
Bloomington, IN 47403
www.authorhouse.com
Phone: 1-800-839-8640

AuthorHouse™ UK Ltd.
500 Avebury Boulevard
Central Milton Keynes, MK9 2BE
www.authorhouse.co.uk
Phone: 08001974150

First published by AuthorHouse 1/24/2007

ISBN: 978-1-4259-9055-8 (sc)

Library of Congress Control Number: 2007900097

Printed in the United States of America
Bloomington, Indiana

This book is printed on acid-free paper.

INTRODUCTION

The way the industry world is going now a days without knowing if the job you have that you may feel is secure, may not be there till it is time for you to retire, or may not be there for you next week. There are no promises with industrial jobs or any job in these times. If your job is gone tomorrow do you know what you will do ahead of time? Don't you think you should prepare something for yourself to fall back on? If your first answer was no, and yes to the second question you picked the right book. This is an easy tounderstand book, it is all in plain everyday talk, written by a plain everyday talking man. It is a good feeling that you will have something to fall back on if you are laid off or your place of employment shuts down, or if you happen to get fired. I am going to show you an easy to learn trade or more or less 3 trades in one. It is a good idea to work part time in some

1

part of this business first to learn more about the work but many people that are confident in themselves just jump right into it. Working for yourself and building up a business on your own is also a good feeling of pride too, and something to be proud about. This book will help you with that confidence. It will be good for you to know that you have the knowledge of a good much needed all over trade, this work is needed in residential homes, also in small and large businesses. With this type of work you can keep your present job and do this on a part time basis. Like I previously said you can work with a Janitorial Service at first cause after reading this book it will give you enough know how to impress your Janitorial Service boss. Later you can make up a name for your business get cards made up. You can choose what you want to do all the services or maybe just concentrate on one or two Janitorial, Floor Maintenance, Carpet Cleaning, Office Cleaning, Home Cleaning, and Window Cleaning. You will like the feeling of later working for yourself in your own business. This is a business you can start out small and slowly build it up and later get people to work for you, or maybe if you want just one person to work with you so the whole work load is not on you. Let me tell you right up front this business is work good honest work. It is not a get rich quick game. Then again you will not really be killing yourself either. You take good care of your customers and they will take care of you. Do a great job for your customers on their floors, or whatever work you are doing for them, and you will have repeat business with them weekly, bi weekly, or monthly whatever the deal is you make between you and the customer. Lot of work I done was just verbal contact and it worked out OK, it is better though to have something in writing especially with the larger businesses. We will first start out learning about many phases of floor care such as stripping and refinishing some people call it waxing, but what we now use on tile is called floor finish. You will be told about general weekly or bi weekly maintenance of floors.

CHAPTER 1

Floor Stripping And Refinishing

In this chapter we are going to discuss Stripping and Waxing/Refinishing on commercial and non commercial floors mainly vinyl, VCT vinyl composition tile. Before you start to strip a floor find out what the floor is made up of and the check your stripper and floor finish containers to check the labels to see if it is good to use the products on the type of floor you are working on. Check to see if there are any loose tiles on the floor you are going to strip cause stripping calls for a lot of solution to be laid down on the floor and the tiles that are loose will come off completely. You can offer to secure the tiles at an extra cost. They may be happy to have you do it. Try to get the tile off without breaking it, if it brakes or it is broke already ask if they have any left over from the job or maybe you can purchase one like it. After you strip the whole floor the floor may match up pretty good with the new tile. That is if you need to put in a new tile in places hopefully you won't have to and hopefully all the tiles will be secure. Use a sharp putty knife and scrape off some of the glue on the bottom of the loose tile and the floor where it is going to go back. Get some floor tile glue and a tile glue spreader and put some glue down on the floor where you are going to put back the tile. When you spread on the glue use the ridged edge of the glue spreader and use a small amount do not go hog wild with the glue. Now wait till the glue gets clear in color and tacky before replacing the tile. We will have to wait till the next day before we strip any section that you just glued back floor tiles.

The first thing we have to know how to do before we start any type of for maintenance project is how to handle the machines. When floor stripping it is best to use a convention floor machine, I prefer an 18 inch in diameter that is a 175 rpm floor machine or a duel speed machine is great to have 175/300, but when stripping just use 175 rpm. The 300 rpm will be good for later for spray buffing floor maintenance. Let's get the hang of using a floor machine, find a wide open space. Make sure no furniture is in your way to break. On a dry tile floor that has been swept well, make sure you have the pad holder on the machine and you can put on a red spray buff pad or a white polishing pad on the bottom of your pad holder. Do not get nervous, you control the machine do not let the machine control you. Hold the handle with both hands and stand close to the handle of the machine. Slowly turn the machine on it may tend to go to the right or left. It is all in the control of the handle. Lightly pull up on the handle it will go in one direction lightly push down on it, it will go in the other direction, keep it steady not up or down but just right in the center the machine will just spin in place now you can try walking with it forwards and backwards and from left to right.

When you start to feel in control and confident in using the floor machine, it may take a couple of hours of practice. Beware when using a buffer make sure your electric cord is always behind you never get it near the pad holder that is turning. Once you get in the groove of handling the machines it will be like riding a bike or putting on shoes.

Ok now you are ready to begin to start stripping and waxing/refinishing that floor like we were planning to do. Take a walk around the floor area that you need to strip, and refinish to see if it has a heavy wax build up, and waxed in dirt, or it may be just an average build up of finish or not much finish at all just a lot of ground in dirt. When you look around and do this you will be able to see how difficult the floor will be to strip. You will be able to figure out your stripping solution mixture, also if you will have to let the solution soak on the floor a few minutes or if you will have to double strip a floor. The majority of floors in a commercial building are made up of commercial VCT vinyl composition tile. Always make sure the stripper and the floor finish you use is safe for the type of floor you are working on 95% of the time it will be ok, but let us be on the safe side and make sure.

Items you are going to need to do a good floor stripping job. A warehouse/ Janitors Broom, this is a good broom to get corners and under furniture like desks if you are working on an office floor. A broom like this usually sells for $6.00 to $7.00 I presently sell them for $6.00 each. It is good to have a soft push broom an 18 or 24 inch wide one they run about $13.50 each with the handle. We are going to need two mop buckets, and one wringer should do it. One bucket will be for the stripper solution, and the bucket with the wringer for clean rinse water and it should be change often. It is good to have a floor squeegee, and a good wet vacuum both these item will help you get the heavy stripper solution off the floor fast and then the floor will be able to rinse easier. The average bucket and wringer combination the cost should run an average of $50.00, and a good wet vacuum or wet dry vacuum shop vacuum about $80.00. All together you should have three mop heads and three mop handles, I would have two 24 oz. cotton mop heads on handles and one rayon 24 oz. mop head on a handle. If the mops are brand new let them soak in some clean water for about an hour prior to using them and then wring them out when you need to start using them. One cotton mop will be for lying down and spreading the stripper solution, the other cotton mop will be used to rinse the floor prior to laying down the sealer/finish solution with the rayon mop; I used rayon because with cotton you can get some lint on the floor when you are applying the finish with a cotton mop. Mop heads run an average cost of $7.00 each wood mop handles are the most economical they cost about $4.75 each.

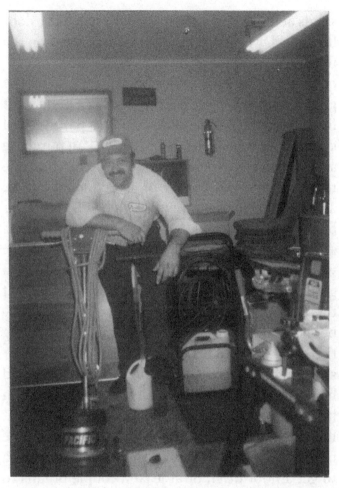

We are going to need floor stripper best to buy it
in a 5 gallon pail non ammoniated, average cost
for a good floor stripper will cost about $50.00
a pail. You are going to need a good floor finish
now a days it is not called wax on tile floors it is
called floor finish, on wood they still use some
waxes and solvents, best to use a finish with high

11

solids about 25% solids that means when the floor finish is dry that percentage of it that stays on the floor dry. Most floor finishes today does not require a coat of floor sealer first if you are using a good floor finish. The average cost of a good floor finish 5 gallon pail goes for $65.00 a pail. Well of course we need a floor machine you can purchase a new one or a used one is good if you can find one maybe in the local paper or search local online. The average cost of a new 18 inch 175 rpm floor buffer will cost about $700.00 with a pad holder. A duel speed buffer 175/300 rpm floor machine would be an estimated cost of $1,000. It is also a good idea to have a can of baseboard stripper if the perimeter of the floor has a say 4 inch rubber baseboard on the bottom of the wall meeting the floor. We will also need a black 18 inch floor stripping pad and a doodlebug rectangular pad holder you put about a 4 inch by 8 inch pad on it, it screws onto a broom handle, you can put it flat on the floor to do corners and also up on the baseboard to get the dirt off them. It is a great idea to get a floor drier, or at least a couple of fans to help the drying time. A new floor drier I believe runs about $200.00.

Say you have floor to do that is heavy soiled and a build up of floor finish on it. Never give a price over the phone bad idea. Go see the floor see how bad it is first, figure how much stripping is involved, how much stripper you will need and how much time you will need to do it. Say this floor we are doing is 2,000 square feet. I am in the state of New Jersey where the cost of living is high. I believe the cost of a floor in this condition should cost the customer $400.00 plus sales tax that makes it .20 cents a square foot. This would include sweeping stripping which you may have to use the whole 5 gallon pail, and 4 coats of floor finish you should have plenty floor finish left over. If you have the same floor to do but it is not quite as in as bad shape then the heavy soiled floor you can charge the customer $ 340.00 plus sales tax that will makes this .17 cents a square foot. A heavy soiled job like this can take two men between 6 to 7 hours, a stripping job the same size but not very heavy build up should take two men about 5 hours to complete.

Let us get ready to do the floor. This is a floor with a lot of heavy build up and waxed in dirt too. After sweeping the whole floor take the bucket that you are going to put the stripper solution in and put about one gallon of stripper in it and two gallons of very hot water, I always preferred hot water the hotter the better to me for stripping a bad floor. Get your rinse bucket and wringer ready with warm rinse water fill it about half way and put one cotton mop in each bucket. Get your floor squeegee and shop vacuum ready and have you floor machine ready with a black stripping pad under your pad holder on the machine. (Work

Step 1) Have the floor machine ready in position to work toward the section you are going to soak with the stripper solution. Never start by having the machine at the far end and laying the stripper down behind the machine. The reason for this is you will have to walk on the soaking stripper while it is loosening up the old dirt and finish to get to your machine and it will be extremely slippery.

Start spreading the floor stripper down at the furthest end of the section you have to strip.

Put the stripper down on an area of about 10 feet by 10 feet also put stripper on the rubber baseboards or use the baseboard spray stripper, now work your machine toward the furthest end have your machine agitate the area before you start to step on the soaked floor it will not be as slippery. Start stripping at the furthest end from left to right and over lap let the machine move slowly as you are stepping backward. Have your person that is working with you use the doodlebug and work on the corners and baseboards.

Once the floor is all machine stripped the guy on the machine should help the guy that is now picking up the stripper by sqee geeing the solution in one spot and wet vacuuming it up and then rinsing the area with the clear water you can also put a little neutral floor cleaner in the pail of rinse water too. When you are ready to do another section back the buffer away about 10 feet or so and spread down some more stripper solution, if the solution ever starts to dry up too fast before you can start machining it just wet it down with some hot water. Keep repeating work step 1 till the whole floor is stripped and rinsed. Get your floor drier or fans in place. Put your machine away, any stripper you may have left, if you have a place to wash out your mops and floor pad and stuff do it, but if you are going to make a mess on the floor you just stripped wash your stuff later at home. Get the rayon mop ready and put about one gallon or more of floor finish in the bucket with the wringer. Start at the left side perimeter up against the baseboard and go all around the perimeter putting the floor finish on the floor nice and evenly, after you got one good coat on the perimeter, now lets go to the far end where we started to strip the floor and start putting the finish down left to right, left to right, make sure you do not get any shoe marks on the floor that was just stripped it is easy to mark up a floor that is freshly stripped without any finish on it to protect it. Put large socks over your shoes if you have to whatever it takes. Take turns putting down the floor finish and one guy can stand back behind and see the way the finish is being applied making sure there are no holidays/missed spots and that it looks even. Position the floor drier, or fans the best way possible so the coats dry right. If you are applying four coats of finish do two coats each if you want. You can strip and refinish a floor yourself but it is a lot of work and time consuming. It is best to do this type of job as a two man operation and if you are doing a larger section then 2000 square feet it can be a three man operation. Keep working till all four coats are applied on the floor, but make sure the floor is completely dry before put on each coat of floor finish. If the customer and you get together on a burnishing deal for I would say at least another $50.00 when the finish sets over a 15 hour period you can go over the floor with a floor burnisher say a 1500 rpm one they run an average of $1,000 for a brand new one the floor will shine like glass and have a wet look to it. Best to use a hi speed hogs hair pad on the pad holder, and when you are done burnishing dust mop the floor with a 24 inch to a 36 inch dust mop. Now a days burnishers are almost a must have in the floor maintenance business. We will talk about floor burnishers a little later on.

CHAPTER 2

General Floor Maintenance How To Keep Up Floors Between Stripping And Refinishing Periods

Let us talk about general maintenance on a floor that was just stripped and finished. It mostly depends on the operation that is going on, on this particular of floor. Suppose it is a medium traffic office area. The floor should be swept with a soft bristle push broom or wide dust mop (oil treated) daily. Twice a week it should be damp mopped with warm water and a little Neutral Floor Cleaner in the pail, and use a clean mop

If this account is only your account for bi weekly or monthly floor maintenance let the customer know what they should do to help the floor hold up at it's best between times before you come in. They most likely won't do it but you can say at least you tried. Then they will look for you to work wonders on the floor when it is time for you to come in to do the floor service.

Suppose it is your first time going in to do this floor since you done the major strip and finish job on it. This floor is in an office area so it shouldn't be so much trouble to keep up and it should not have to be stripped and refinish but once a year. If it were a bar, luncheonette, or a cafeteria these kinds of floors get beat and are harder to keep up you get a lot of spills, and grease problems and should have once a week maintenance in my book and have a major strip and refinish job twice a year. Let us get back to dealing with the office floor, Sweep or dust mop it well damp mop it with a neutral cleaner in the bucket of warm water, check to see if there are any marks in the floor like shoe marks if so get your 175 rpm machine or if you have a 175 /.300 duel speed machine and a spray bottle full of spray buff. Spray buff can be purchased by the gallon or by the case 4/1 gallon per case average cost about $9.00 a gallon. Now you will need a Red spray buff pad under your machine. Set your spray bottle so the solution comes out more or less like a light mist. Spray across an area that got marks on it and that seems to have had heavy traffic since you done the strip job. Now take your machine with the Red pad under it go from left to right across a row of tiles now go right to left over the set of tiles to the rear of the first set of tiles you went over the first time, now go forward left to right over the set of tiles you went over the first time the shine should come back after all the spray buff solution is now buffed out. Repeat this procedure till you are done with all the marked up sections of floor if you have a duel speed machine use 300 rpm for spray buffing, turn your red pad over several times during spray buffing the side of the pad toward the machine will heat up and you will be able to scrap off the dust easily. When you are done with this get your wide dust mop and dust mop all what we call "waxing dust" up. Sweep it in a dust pan and throw it out. A hi speed burnisher has four wheels two rear wheels on it to wheel the machine from place to place. The other two wheels stay on the floor when you are burnishing. You have to adjust the handle into position so the machine will feel comfortable for you to operate. The two wheels that are closest to the pad holder stay on the floor and when you turn the machine on keep the pad holder and pad off the floor as the machine speeds up all the way, lightly let the pad come in contact with the floor and move the machine back and fourth on the wheels as you have the pad lightly touching the floor. If you pull up on the handle it will put more pressure on the pad so be careful not to put too much pressure on the front of the machine and pad and floor. It may make burn marks on the floor, most of the times some spray buff solution and lightly going over the areas with the burnisher will take these marks out. High speed burnisher with a hi speed hogs hair pad and high speed burnish the whole floor you can use some spray buff mist here and there as you burnish the whole floor. The pad holder usually always comes with a burnisher already attached. When finished burnishing the whole floor dust mop it carefully.

Chapter 3

More Ways To Maintain Floors Between Major Stripping Jobs

Suppose it is time again to go maintain the floor again that we performed that major stripping job on. We are going to do everything the same as we did in chapter 2 till it is time to hi speed burnish. Before burnishing we are going to get a clean bucket and wringer and clean rayon mop head. WE are going to use a product that is called a Restorer, or it may be called Floor Restorer many different chemical manufacturers make this product. The cost of this product is about $15.50 a gallon. Read the label carefully it will tell you how many parts restorer to how many parts water. Mix the restorer and the water in the bucket. Ok let us start at the far end and start mopping the restorer on the floor, and do not forget to get the floor drier or the fans to help the drying process. When the floor is dry to a haze you can start to burnish it out, when done burnishing take the wide dust mop and dust mop the whole floor. The cost to keep up this 2000 square foot floor and maintain it once a week to me should be in 2006 in NJ should be $120.00 and tax, every two weeks I would say $140.00 and tax and once every four weeks $160.00. I did not say anything about doing the floor every three weeks cause when you start building up a good business and setting up your jobs every 3 week jobs is odd and may cause it to be difficult to book your jobs.

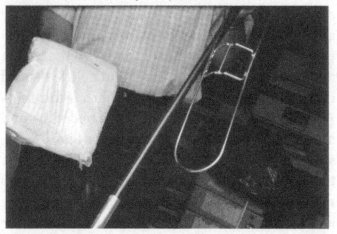

Here is another way to maintain the floor maybe after it had a lot of traffic and the first layer of floor finish is getting dirty and wear is starting to show. Get you conventional floor machine ready. Sweep the whole floor do a good sweeping job. Bring in two buckets and one wringer and two cotton mops and handles and one rayon mop and handle. Get a good floor cleaner like Mr. Clean is good read the mixing directions and put it in the bucket without the wringer. You will need a green sometimes they are blue conventional floor scrubbing pad. Now you do the floor scrubbing almost the same exact way you done the stripping procedure, but you do not have to put the scrubbing solution down as heavy as you did with the stripper solution. We should not have to get out the wet vacuum, maybe just the sqee gee so you can push the solution to one section on the floor after it is scrubbed with the machine. Then you can rinse and pick up the solution with the bucket and wringer with warm water and a little neutral cleaner in the water use the other cotton mop. Add more scrubbing solution when necessary and also change your pick up rinse water often. Make sure you have your floor drier in place. When the floor is completely dry get your rayon mop ready and rinse out the bucket and wringer pour about one gallon of floor finish in the bucket with the wringer and start applying it to the floor the same way you put on the first coat of finish after

24

you stripped the floor. This should bring the floor back looking great. Try if you can to have you customer to agree on having their floor maintenance done once a week or once every two weeks, I believe once a month is too much of a gap. It is all going to be on you I do not believe they are ever going to damp mop themselves and if they do they will most likely use the wrong cleaning stuff, they might just sweep if they have to.

The week after you done the initial stripping job you may get away with just using a wide dust mop and sweeping the floor with it, them damp mopping with a cotton mop head, bucket and wringer with neutral cleaner and warm water in the bucket, and then spray buff with the spray bottle set to a mist and just us the burnisher on the whole floor and squirt a little spray buff on it where you feel it is needed. Ok now you have four ways you can keep up the floor after you done an initial first cleaning of stripping and refinishing. So when you come in after whatever it will be weekly, bi weekly, or monthly you got a good idea what you have to do. I am sure as you go along in the floor maintenance business you will find your own personal way of maintaining the floors. Offices are great to do floors, remember bars get pretty bad try to get them weekly if you want to deal with them, and small food places you got to deal with grease if you need the work do them if not stay away take it from my experience.

CHAPTER 4

Cleaning And Waxing Wood Floors

Years back when I done wood floors and floor waxing people still use this method today. Try to stay away from water on wood as much as you can if you can. I would sweep the floor and take my conventional 175 rpm floor machine and take an old dry floor pad and make my own pad with number 2 steel wool or you can buy number 2 steel wool pads already made up and put it on top of the old pad and take a scrapper and put some wax into the steel wool pad to start. Get yourself white emulsion paste wax and yellow solvent wax use more of the yellow that works best on wood floors. (To make your own steel wool pad by yourself a roll of steel wool number 2 because 3 is a little too course. Put on a pair of work gloves start taking the steel wool off the roll and start a twisting motion with it as you are putting it on the top side of the old pad on the floor, start unraveling the steel wool and keep twisting it till the old pad is covered with the steel wool tuck the end piece of the steel wool between the pad and under the steel wool, it is cheaper to make up tour own pads to cut the steel wool use a sharp tin snip or a heavy pair of scissors. Some guys would put their foot on the end and twist the roll and tear it, not me this stuff cuts you if you are not safe,) With the wax on the pad turn the pad over steel wool and wax part on the floor put your pad holder on top and machine on top of the pad holder till it clicks in place adjust the handle and start spreading the wax across the floor evenly do not over apply wax to the floor cause it may become too slippery. To add wax where you need it have a small pail with more yellow then white wax in it mix it up a little apply it right on the floor with a scrapper then move near it with your machine running towards the right side of you machine heading for it and when you get right next to the wax clump on the floor with your right hand lift up on your machine just a little with the machine still running all the while and go right on top of that wax and keep spreading it evenly on the floor. When you are done applying wax to the whole floor remove the steel wool and pad and either put a number 2 steel wool pad on the old floor pad and put it steel wool part against the wood floor or make up a pad from a roll of steel wool and put it steel wool side on the floor and then put the pad holder and machine evenly on the pad and start to buff up the floor. When the whole floor is buffed out take the wide oil treated clean dust mop the whole floor in a sweeping motion.

Another way you can do a wood floor is with a wood and gym finish it will most likely be less slippery if done this way. This wood floor finish is very high in solids. If the floor is dirty first sweep it with either a push broom or the wide dust mop. You may have to damp mop it with a neutral cleaner added to the water. You may have to lightly scrub the floor "not too much water" put down with the mop a little water with the neutral cleaner take the conventional machine and scrub over the floor lightly with a number 2 steel wool pad under the machine or a pad that you made yourself. Do a section at a time and pick up the water with a mop and wring it out and then rinse the whole floor. You can use a fan or a floor drier to speed up the drying process. With an applicator or a rayon mop evenly apply the wood and gym finish one gallon covers 500 square feet. One or two coats may be sufficient. This product can be purchased in 5 gallon pails. If a wood floor is scratched and worn down it may be necessary for whoever is in charge of the place to have the floor sanded and refinished. Sometimes just cleaning and waxing/finishing the floor will not do the trick if they are in very bad shape. I done floor sanding and refinishing before, but I do not recommend you to do it. It can interfere with your jobs and really has nothing to do with the Janitorial trade it is another ballgame I would leave it to the floor sanders.

CHAPTER 5

Giving Estimates On Floor
Stripping
And Refinishing
And General Cleaning
And Waxing/refinishing
Also Wood Floor Cleaning
And Waxing/finishing

Let us look at giving prices to customers that
have 1000 square feet of tile floors that have to be
stripped and refinished with four to five coats of
finish. One thousand square feet of floor in bad

shape should cost the customer New Jersey price $200.00 plus sales tax. If you have to move furniture around you have to charge extra. One man on a job should average $35.00 if you have a helper working with you and you are liable for the two man operation should average $60.00 an hour. If the place has a lot of furniture that they are going to want you to buggy lug back and forth that takes almost double the time to do the floor cause you may have to do it in sections. It all depends on the situation that you are in

A one thousand square foot floor that is not quite as bad should cost the customer $170.00 plus sales tax. Do not forget to charge extra for buggy lugging. You are in the floor business not the moving business "Beware there are a lot of people that will try to take advantage of your good nature out there". Being too good hearted with them is not going to put food on you table. I am telling you because I made these mistakes. Be on the watch for people that try to add in extra work too!

The average cost of bi weekly that is once every two weeks floor cleaning and waxing, or spray buffing and burnishing keep up for 1000 square feet of floor should cost the customer $100.00 a little more for monthly and say $80.00 for a weekly service. Now if the floors you do are less then 1000 square, oh yes get yourself a floor measurer it is on one or two wheels and you start at one wall and go to the opposite end and add 6 inches say that is the length and now you measure the width and when to come to the end of the wall add 6 inches to the total width. Multiply the length times the width and to get the square footage.

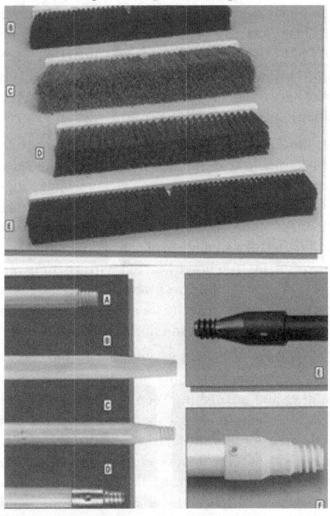

Under 1000 square feet you will be cheating your-self if you charge the same way as 1000 square feet or more. Let us say someone called you to strip and refinish a room 10X12 which is 120 square feet you can not charge 17 cents or 20 cents a square foot. At 20 cents a square foot that would come to only $24.00. This type of small room or office you got to figure time and material some-times the small jobs are more work, believe it. I would say a floor like this to strip and refinish should cost your customer $85.00 plus tax and $40.00 for the general floor keep up every 2 weeks or once a month $45.00 plus tax.

Wood floors the ways I told you in the last chap-ter, to do them for 1000 square should cost your customer $120.00 plus tax this is based on 12 cents a square foot that is doing it the paste wax way. Using the wood floor gym finish you will have to charge about $200.00 or more because this stuff is expensive. Any less then 1000 square feet you have to charge accordingly, such as how much work is involved. A 10X12 room 120 square feet with the paste wax method should cost your customer about $35.00 plus tax the same floor with the liquid finish method should cost your customer about $50.00 plus tax.

Concrete floors can be stripped or you can use a floor all purpose cleaner and degreaser with a black stripping pad and do it in the same manner that you would strip or scrub a tile floor. When it dries you would put on a coat of concrete floor sealer, it comes in clear and in colors too. This sealer may be expensive, when you give your bid take cost of the sealer into consideration.

This concludes the chapters on floor maintenance, when you are called upon to do one I hope now you have a good understanding on what to do on a floor when you are called upon to do one. If you feel you may be interested in some extra help and maybe someone to answer some questions you have go toward the end of this book.

CHARTER 6

Carpet Cleaning Methods

Carpet cleaning this is another business in itself. There is a lot of work in this business both in residential and commercial. The machines to do carpets are rotary shampooers, you can take your conventional 175 rpm floor machine and buy a plastic shampoo tank and a hose should come with it and a fitting. The tank clamps to the handle of the machine with two nuts on each clamp there are two clamps. On the deck of your buffer you will see a round plug that can be removed so the hose from the tank can go though it with the fitting attachment. A shampoo tank like this goes for about $80.00. You will need a shower feed shampoo brush they come in wood, plastic, and aluminum backings. I liked the plastic, because the wood warps and the aluminum is too expensive. The plastic shower feed brush in an 18 inch diameter costs about $100.00 to $150.00 and fits right under your machine like a pad holder. You can also do this on a duel speed 175/300 rpm floor machine, but I would just use the 175 rpm speed while doing carpet shampooing. The average price for a gallon of rug shampoo cost is about $14.00 a gallon and you get 4 gallons in a case if you buy it by the case. Just read the mixing directions on the shampoo bottle. First thing you want to do is vacuum the carpet, it may be hard to get close to the edges and corners when vacuuming so I used to use a hard bristle broom and brush out all the dust and dirt in all the corners and edges, and then look for spots, get yourself a good spot remover and small spot scrubbing brush and have lots of white rags on hand for blotting the spot after you spray the spot remover on it and scrub it with the brush, then you dab it with a white rag or towel and it should pick a lot of the spot up onto the rag. A low pile carpet should come out well with doing it with the rotary carpet scrubbing described here. Put the solution into the tank pull the handle on the tank gently so some solution goes to you shower feed brush and start scrubbing a 4 foot by 4 foot section at a time till you are done. For a low pile carpet this method should good enough.

We used to use a two step carpet cleaning method the floor machine as a rotary shampooer, and a carpet extractor with a wand. We made sure to vacuum the carpet good spot clean the carpet you can also spray the carpet with a traffic lane pre spotter, and now start shampooing with the rotary shampooer. Get the carpet extractor set up put extraction cleaner and hot water in the solution area read the mixing directions. In the recovery part of the machine you can put in a little defoamer and as you are extracting the carpet add some as needed. When I used to do carpets with this two step method I never used a defoamer. If you have another person with you one can use the floor machine as a shampooer, and when that person gets enough done you can start with the extractor but make sure not to be in each others way. Go over the sections that were done with the shampooer with the extractor. This method may be a little time consuming, but the carpet comes out very clean even with a high pile. Most portable extractors come with two vacuum motors have the both turned on for a deep down clean carpet. You can pick up a decent new portable commercial carpet extractor for about $1000.

You can also do carpets with a portable extractor that is a self contained commercial carpet extractor. This type of extractor is has a motorized brush built in with it. This type of machine does a great job, but it is not as easy as getting around with a wand, with the wand you can get under and around things easier. The average cost for a carpet machine similar to this one I just described would go for about $1,650.00. With this machine you just vacuum the carpet first and you scrub and extract all in one step. My vacuum of choice is a good commercial upright, that is just my choice, you may prefer a backpack vacuum or canister vacuum all are good. I use to have a magnet screwed to the front of my uprights to pick up the staples and paper clips before they can get caught up in my vacuum.

If you want to go big in carpet cleaning and way out you can get a truck mounted unit, extraction method. The only thing you bring in from the unit is the hose and the wand. Most of these units have upholstery attachments too; you can get upholstery attachments for portable machines too. Upholstery cleaning is a business by itself. The truck mount machine new average cost is about $8,500.00 it is something you would have to think about. I done furniture with a hand held brush with a pail of shampoo for hard to get out spots and a hand upholstery tool attached to a portable extractor.

You can run a good special for homes 2 rooms and a hallway say $69.95 make up fliers and put a small add in the local paper. Includes vacuuming, spot remover for stains "never guarantee that every stain will come out" machine clean the carpets, deodorize them and use a carpet protector. You can purchase a very inexpensive carpet protector that mixes with water and you can put it in a garden sprayer. When running a special just use the inexpensive protector because some carpet protectors can really cost. If a customer calls for a certain brand protector you will have to charge them for it. When mixing the water with the protector use a lot less water then it calls for because you are going to be putting it on the carpet when it is still wet anyway.

Take an average carpeted room and clean the carpet the same way as we described it above a room about 14 X 16 like about an average size living room vacuumed, spot remover, machine cleaned 2 step or one step method with a extractor with a built in brush, or truck mount carpet cleaning machine, deodorized, and an inexpensive carpet protector premixed in a garden sprayer. You should charge your customer $40.00 to $45.00 for a room done this size and done this way this is a very fair price. Take an area of carpeting 1000 or more square feet a fare price would be 15 cents a square foot. Sometimes you may find chewing gum on a carpet it is a hard thing to remove sometimes, they make an aerosol spray called something like carpet gum remover it freezes the gum but you still have to scrap it off the best you can.

There is another way to maintain carpets that works good on high traffic areas like entrance ways and hallways. It is called bonnet cleaning. This is a round bonnet that goes under your shampoo brush or pad holder. You soak the bonnet in a shampoo and hot water solution and wring it out and put it under your machine and go over a section of carpet then go soak the bonnet and wring it out and keep repeating the same way till you are done. Here is an important helpful hint;

some tips on your furniture may leave rusts spots on your carpet and some wood furniture if it was stained with a water base may tend to run on a damp carpet. Make up or you can buy small plastic square coasters and put it under the legs of the furniture that may be harmful to the carpet, or the damp carpet may be harmful to the furniture. You may also use a floor dryer to speed up the drying process on the carpeting. Carpets should be vacuumed often to help keep them clean and to keep lot of deep down dirt from building up.

Well this just about covers what you may need to know on carpet cleaning methods. I hope you have a good understanding about cleaning carpets with these methods. If you feel you may be interested in extra help someone to help you with some questions you may have or talk shop with you see the page towards the end of this book.

CHAPTER 7

Janitorial/General Cleaning Maintenance Office Cleaning Plus

I have done many office cleaning jobs on my own and also for janitorial services I worked for. Most of the offices I cleaned were on the main floor which to me is better. It is good this way cause less buggy lugging and saves steps. When you are giving an estimate on office cleaning there is a lot you have to take into consideration number 1 how large is the area you are cleaning, measure it for square footage cause you will be vacuuming and sweeping and mopping theses areas. How many bathrooms you are going to be cleaning? If you are going to be the one supplying the paper towels and toilet tissue bill them separate for this and be sure you compensate yourself a few bucks extra for your trouble of running around and picking the stuff up and delivering it to the job. "I have to tell you by experience do not give your work away, do not low ball estimates just to get a job it is not worth it. I have been down that road when I was young. Think of your customers and treat them right but do not mix your business with friends. They are not your friends they are your bread and butter and please remember this. I wrote this book so you people do not make mistakes in this field like I did". How many desks stations are going to be in the office area? This way you will know how many trash cans will have to be emptied and how many desks have to be dusted, and phones wiped down. Does this office have a snack area that you have to clean? I would supply liners for the desk trash cans with the estimate and also the large ones that I will be taking out the trash with. I would also include with the price all of my cleaning chemicals bathroom cleaners, polishes, floor cleaners, etc. Windows outside and inside are most likely not going to be done as often as the office cleaning so that will be a separate estimate. The only glass that should be done every time you clean is the main entrance door and area. The liners you will most likely need for the desk trash cans would be the 8 to 10 gallon ones they are 24

X 24 6 micron in clear 1000 liners per case and run about $18.00 per case.

When giving an estimate you have to keep into consideration how often is the general cleaning going to take place. Most busy offices may need the service done every day or 5 days a week, some offices are done 3 or 2 nights a week. I had two that we done once a week but to me that is letting it go a little too far, the workers were piling up their trash by the back door and I had to bust my hump making 2 or 3 trips to the dumpster even before empting the desk trash cans that were all just about full from the work week. The other office I done once a week the bathrooms got pretty messy even the floors and a lot of stuff on the carpet. When you are giving an office cleaning estimate most of the time it will be based on a monthly estimate or once every 4 weeks. Things like carpet cleaning should be billed extra when they need to have it done or when they ask about having the carpet cleaned, or you can approach them about it. Floor cleaning and finishing is also extra.

Here is an example someone calls you for an estimate that has two bathrooms a lady's room has one stall and a sink and is not too large just average size, the men's room has a sink, one stall and a urinal. The first time I would concentrate on cleaning the walls too they are mainly ceramic tile in most office bathrooms. The main office area has 8 desks and there are 5 single offices with one desk each around the perimeter of the main open section. The place has a small counter area behind the counter is a refrigerator a microwave. The whole area is wall to wall carpeted. "Let the people know what you are going to include in your estimate for general cleaning and what is going to be charged separate like the windows, carpet cleaning, you can ask if they are going to want you to supply them with things like toilet tissue and paper towels hand soap etc. all this would be a separate invoice to eliminate confusion and problems in the future. When you give your estimate on general office cleaning that is what you are going to do just the general office maintenance, the only windows that you should have to do every time is the front door area not the whole place that is why all the windows if there is a lot of them and you are to do them in and out is going to take some time and should be billed when you do them as a separate job". The general office cleaning usually would be cleaning the bathrooms, dust and polish the desks if possible and wipe off the phones. Clean the counter and clean around the food area and clean the main door glass empty trash and change the dirty liners and vacuum carpets.

The materials you should have on hand if you get this account is a 44 gallon container with a dolly that fits on the bottom of the container so you can push it around when you pick up the trash and a Caddy Bag or Rim Caddy to hold your cleaning supplies and trash liners 40 X46 heavy duty which is 40 to 45 gallon bags or better to have a larger one which would be 43 X 47.You will need a good commercial upright vacuum or back pack vacuum cleaner. You are going to need a broom, mop bucket and wringer, a duster, rags, all purpose cleaner, pine cleaner, bathroom cleaner, toilet bowl brushes, spray bottles, window cleaner, and small trash can liners, also I would get some of them cleaning and polishing disposable wipes.

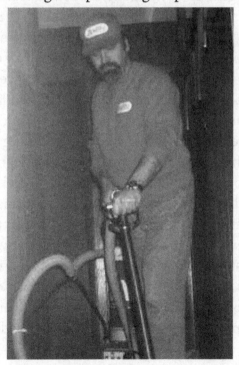

Let us talk about giving an estimate on the office area we discussed in this chapter. Suppose we are going to do this office cleaning twice a week. It should take one man less then two hours and two men about one hour each cleaning. I would charge an average of $65.00 per cleaning, if they only want the service once a week I would charge $80.00 per cleaning. I would bill them every 4 weeks for a once a week cleaning the invoice would be $320.00 plus tax for four services. Twice a week the invoice would be $520.00 plus tax for eight services. You can use your own judgment on how to give an estimate if they need the service three times a week or daily. Try your best to get a key for yourself so you can do the place after office hours or early in the morning before they open. I used to have keys to about half of my places and I was not bonded but in the mid 80's I had liability insurance (We will talk about the insurance later) It can be hard on you and your scheduling of jobs when you got to do an office by waiting for someone to open for you and you have to work by their time. I had a lot of experience with not having a key. Sometimes the person would show up late and then I had to rush a job because the workers would start to come in and we would get in each others way, worse yet sometimes the person that was suppose to open the door for me would not show up at all and then you got to reschedule the job and that can make a mess of things, so try your best at getting your own key.

When it comes time to do the windows the customer may want them cleaned inside and out say once a month. Some customers may want you to do the outside more often then the inside. If the outside is just to be done charge half as much as inside and outside. Average store front and large office window panes are about 4 ft. X 8ft. I would say the average price to charge to clean a window like this inside and out with a window wash brush or window wash applicator and squeegee would be $5.00. So count them up and give your estimate. Take into consideration doors and also some windows may be different in size. We will talk a little more about window washing later.

If you wish to start up a home cleaning business you can do that, my sister done some domestic cleaning. I really never went into home cleaning I just done carpet cleaning and floor maintenance and windows in homes. I believe once I had one house but I did not keep it too long. People may be very particular when it comes to their homes and sometimes their may be no satisfying them. If you want to clean residential homes do not let me stop you, you may get some good customers I am just expressing my opinion on domestic cleaning. This just about covers it up for this chapter I hope it helps you with general cleaning and office cleaning. If you need more help or someone to talk things over with see the end of the book under the heading "The Club".

CHAPTER 8

Ways to Earn Extra Money and Some Cleaning Tips

Take a look at the type of customers you got so far. Now you do not have to do this cause you know how some people can be, some people want the best quality items and a bargain too, stay away from them. In other words they want Scott paper products at no frills paper products prices. I catered to people like this and tried to make them happy do not ask me why I did it. You can never make them happy. I had to be stupid to waste valuable time on them. I am telling you do not make my mistakes you are in business to make money not to try to pamper penny wise customers. Suppose you do floors and/or windows in a food place maybe you can ask them if they need napkin holders, or napkins, place mats, paper plates, food to go containers, etc. This is a good means of extra income. If you get a few customers that want to get supplies then you can look into becoming a distributor now this is another business all in itself. You contact a wholesaler in some cases a manufacturer that just sells to distributors and not the end user. You will be the one selling to the end user. If you do office cleaning they may need air fresheners in the bathrooms, hand soap, toilet tissue, paper towels, etc. Some places may even want to buy new mop heads so they can keep up their floors. Trash liners may be a big item for their business and even at their home. If you do some floor maintenance your customers may need an entrance mat at the main entrance. They may need a 3X5 or a 4X6 or a 3X10 whatever it may be. Some places have more then one entrance you may be selling them 3 mats who knows. These mats usually have a carpeted nap with a non slip vinyl backing. The customers are going to need someone to clean these mats for them. Now it is going to take some time till they dry so they should have a back up of mats because you can not put them back the one that is still damp. Another thing you can think about is a mat cleaning and rental service for your customers, every two weeks or so put down a clean mat and take away the dirty one to be cleaned. In this case you will have to purchase the mats and the customers will pay the rental cleaning service to you. I would say a 3X5 mat changed every two weeks with a clean one should cost the customer $6.00 plus tax, larger mats extra, if they want you to change it every week you can charge about $1.00 less per mat.

What I also done for a while for a couple bar and grills and a luncheonette where I done the floors was clean the grill hood filters. I used a strong degreaser and let them soak and them pressure washed them in my driveway. That was a lot of years ago I would guess you have to charge at least $5.00 or more each or it is not worth it.

Window washing with a window brush and squeegee and extension handles. If you are doing a storefront or office front window about 4 X 10 feet have your window washing pail with widow cleaning solution and maybe a little vinegar and ammonia in the water. Put your window brush in the solution and have the brush attached to your extension handle and start at the top and work you way down the glass brushing the solution over the whole window. Now take your sqee gee which is made up of a rubber blade, a channel and a small handle and put it on you extension handle. Start at the top left and tilt the sqee gee a little to the right as you are working the sqee gee down the glass and stop about two feet before the bottom of the window pane. You should always have a towel to wipe the sqee gee blade off each time you do a section of the glass, keep going till you are done with the upper part of the glass. You can do the bottom half or the 2 feet that is left by holding the sqee gee vertically and start at the left and work your way all the way to the end of the glass on the right. Wipe the bottom window frame off with your towel. When the weather was very cold when I had windows to do I used to use a lot of automobile windshield wash all seasons brand in my window washing solution bucket to keep the windows from freezing up. Always have clean rags and/or towels with you on the jobs. It is good to have about three different size sqee gee assembles 12 inch 18 inch and 24 inch are good sizes to have on hand. Later when you start doing windows you will be able to judge the sizes you are going to want on hand based on the type of windows you are doing. This just about wraps it up for this chapter on Ways to Earn Extra Money and Some Cleaning Tips. I hope you learned something in this chapter. If you need some help with some question you need answered I will try to help to the best of my ability. Go towards the end of this book to the section that explains the Club.

CHAPTER 9

Getting Your Own Business Started

Here are a few things you should know before starting your own Janitorial business. Make up a business name for yourself and go have it registered with the county clerk office. The best thing to do is get a lawyer and register your business as a corporation or an LLC or an LP or whatever he may suggest that is best for you. This may cost you $300 to $400 depending on what lawyer charges for this. You will also have to apply for a sales tax certificate of authority state ID tax number. You are going to need a good running commercial vehicle for you business say a full sized van with commercial insurance on it. You can most likely be able to get a half way decent used van for $3,500.00, in 1983 I bought a 71 Chevy Van for $250.00 I do not suggest you do this cause the customers saw me coming and it was not a good advertisement of my work. I bought this van when I stopped the business for a while and was going to go back into it again because I had a family and needed extra money besides the job I had. In about 8 months part-time in my business I was getting about the same as my 40 hour a week job paid. Have your van lettered with your phone number or if it has windows you can put stick on letters yourself or you can get magnetic signs made up. The business name what are your services and your phone number. You should also get general liability business insurance with what is called completed operations tell the insurance company, if they ask, you only do about 5% floor cleaning and waxing/finishing. I was doing floors with paste wax if you put down too much tends to be a little slippery I guess that is why it is not used too much anymore. I was doing a floor in a store 23 years ago I was not carrying liability insurance what happened 2 days after I was done with the floor I wasn't even there, a woman slipped, I did not find out till 1 year and 7 months later. I received a letter to go to court. I was only doing this work at the time to supplement my income. I had to pay my lawyer $1,100 to go to court for me I was shaking. After all was said and done the store's insurance decided to pay her claim. The next day I looked into getting liability business insurance I got a combined van and business commercial liability policy based on a one man operation with completed operations for $2,300.00 I would say today you can get the same type of policy for about $3,000. If you have a person working for you on the books you may need to look into work mans compensation you may be able to get it from the same company but when they know you have a person working for you the liability may go up or you can tell them only one man works at a time, I do not know how that will go over though. The offices I done always would ask for a certificate of insurance from time to time. If you start a partnership I am not positive but I do not think work mans compensation is mandatory but I would always have general liability. The insurance money is not all to be paid up front I believe you will need a third down and the money for the van and lawyer to register the business so that would be $4,800.00 so far and then figure out your equipment that you are going to want to start out with. You can start out with floor maintenance and janitorial and go into carpet cleaning with upholstery somewhere down the road when you start to make some money. To start yourself out in Floor Maintenance and Janitorial with new equipment with one conventional machine and one burnisher, cleaning supplies and brooms, dust mop and a bucket and wringer combo, mops and window cleaning equipment should cost you about $2,200.00, so your total as of now is $7,000 and say about $100.00 or so to register the vehicle. Later down the road you can add on the carpet and upholstery cleaning for about $1,500 if you later want a pressure washer they go for about $400.00. You may want a business phone and advertise in the yellow pages this would be monthly payment and the yellow pages is good advertising, and advertise on your van and get business cards you can get 1000 for about $30.00. Buy yourself a ledger to keep the dates and records of you income, and save all the recites when you buy supplies for the business and keep track of your mileage on the business vehicle and costs of all insurance you will need this when you do your taxes. So I say for about $10,000 take or give a few hundred you are on your way in a good business. It will not be a picnic, it is good honest work and you don't have to worry about getting laid off cause you are not going to lay yourself off. Try contacting a lot of lodges and clubs like the Moose Lodge, Elks Lodge, Knights of Columbus, VFW Halls, and American Legions you do not have to be a member to get a lot of good work from theses type of places. Sometimes they rather hire outsiders. Good Luck to you all.

PLEASE NOTE

Please let it be known the author of this book Richard S. Takasch or Bud's Maintenance Service Company, LLC is not responsible or is not liable for anything in this book that may be misinterpreted by the reader. We also are not responsible for any mistakes the reader or any of his workers or partners may make while doing any of the jobs that are explained in this book. We will not be liable for any bodily injury or death while the readers of this book or his helpers or partners are performing any of the jobs described in this book. We will not accept any responsibility for the way the said reader of this book maintains and runs his business. We the author will not be liable for the reader not inquiring about proper insurance that he is responsible to have while running his or her business. This book was written to give the reader General information to help them to acquire some knowledge of the Janitorial trade and ideas on how they can start a business. Nothing written in this book is scribed in stone.

Thank You,

Richard S. Takasch (Author)

THE CLUB

Hello dear buyers of this book I would like to do my best in answering any questions you may have to do with the Janitorial Business/Trade I was a member of CMI for about 3 years that is Cleaning Maintenance Institute the wrote suggestions on what to do to make things run smoother many of my ideas were printed in their forum sections of their magazine called CM cleaning & maintenance management.. Someone in the business asked me about his mops in the winter got stiff and stuck to the metal sides of his van or to the floor. I told him to attach a dowel a thick one like you would find in your clothes closet that you put your hangers on, and affix it no less then 2 feet from the floor of the van. I had mine towards the back but you can put your wherever you like as long as your mop handle can lay out without interfering with anything. I averaged about 4 mops in my van most of the time and you can let them hang over this pole and they will not touch anything. They will freeze but not stick to any of the other equipment or to each other just keep then spaced apart.

The club is a way you can talk to me and I will answer your questions the best I know how and try to help you along. I will give you a toll free number to call. You can call 10 AM to 6 PM eastern time Monday – Friday just once a week please, but I will give you a e-mail address also if you happen to need a little help on something you can e-mail me up to twice a week. You will have an ID number so when you call just give me your name and assigned ID number. When you e-mail me put your name and ID number in the subject and I will answer your e-mail as soon as possible. Here is how to sign up for the club, you can sign up for one or two years. One year would be $59.95 plus tax two year would be $99.95 plus tax. It is well worth the cost. Once every two months I will send you out my newsletter about the Janitorial and things related to it. You can pay by credit card Visa, Master Card, Discover, American Express, or you can pay by check or money order. The total for one year would cost.

$59.95

$99.95

4.20 7% sales tax Total for two Years 7.00 7% sales tax

$64.15 Total $106.95 Total

If you are paying by credit card Fax or Mail your credit card information.

Type of credit card Visa, Master Card, Discover, Am Ex

Expiration Date of the card – Please provide a phone number if I need to get in touch with you

Complete your name and address with zip code where the bills go for this credit card

Let me know where you will want your ID number, toll free number, e-mail address, and newsletter sent to if it is not the same as the credit card billing address

Mail this to Bud's Maintenance,LLC Or fax to 1 732 382-3949

42 Park Ave.

Iselin, NJ 08830

If you are going to send a check or money order make the check out to

Bud's Maintenance,LLC and send it with your name address and phone number to

Bud's Maintenance,LLC

42 Park Ave.

Iselin, NJ 08830

NOTES

NOTES

About the Author

Hello my name is Richard S. Takasch known to most people as "Buddy" I am the Registered Agent and partner of Bud's Maintenance Service Company, L.L.C. Janitorial Supplies and Janitorial Paper Products. I started in the Janitorial Trade in 1972. I worked part time for two Janitorial Services. One of the services contracted a large plant that I worked in 4 ½ hours an evening I done general office cleaning and Spray Buffed floors the other Janitorial Service I worked for I done General Office cleaning for two small companies. It took about a little over an hour an evening. I was in my senior year of high school back then. In the year 1973 I got a good job rotating shifts in a chemical factory in Sayreville NJ. I purchased 17 inch in diameter American Lincoln floor machine brand new for $300.00. In the early 70's many of the floor waxers used paste wax, and made up their own floor pads from rolls of steel wool. They used a steel wool pad for applying the paste was and a clean steel wool pad for buffing it out. While working in the plant I picked up a few accounts and done some floor waxing jobs on the side. Most of the jobs were bi weekly/once every two weeks. I used paste wax on tile floors back then. First I had to do a good sweeping job then damp mop the floor with a Neutral Cleaner before I paste waxed and buffed the floor then I would dust mop the floor with a 2 foot wide dust mop. I have done a few taverns and luncheonettes in the start of my business. In 1975 I was laid off from my regular job. I then made up business cards and passed them around telling that I done floor maintenance and store front window cleaning. After about a 2 year lay off I got called back to my factory job. It did not last to long for me in 1978 it was over. I added carpet cleaning to my part time business as I also worked for other established Janitorial businesses at the same time. I worked full time in other factory jobs thinking that I may find a secure one. In the mean time I also worked for other janitorial services on a part time basis. I keep on working on my own service till I built it up till I felt it would be secure enough alone without the need of another job, and would be able to go it alone with just the Janitorial Business. I then added Carpet Cleaning to my offered services. In the late 80's and early 90's I was a member of CMI Cleaning Maintenance Institute they printed some of my ideas in the monthly magazine. In the early 90's I belonged to the local Chamber of Commerce. My only regret is I should have started in my own business and got it off the ground sooner then I did. I have a total of about 30 years working in the Janitorial trade. I am now presently a Supply Distributor.

Made in United States
Orlando, FL
10 July 2024

48802794R00046